Beach Cocktails

75 Drinks, Tiki Cocktails And Snacks To Savor At The Beach Or Anywhere

DOUGLAS SHAW

DEDICATION

To Friends and lovers of the tropics!

TABLE OF CONTENTS

INTRODUCTION 1

  Types Of Cocktail Glasses 2

  Cocktail Bar Utensils 3

CLASSIC TIKI 5

  Mai Tai 5

  Fog Cutter 6

  Rum Swizzle 7

  Painkiller 8

  Scorpion 9

  Planters Punch 10

  Zombie 11

  The Saturn 12

  The Ancient Mariner 13

RUM 14

  Cranberry Zombie 14

  Pina Colada 15

  Mojito 16

  Strawberry Daiquiri 17

  Caribbean Rum Punch 18

  Bushwacker 19

  Hurricane 20

  Dirty Banana 21

  Rum Sunset 22

VODKA 23

Bloody Mary 23

Ice Blue Martini 24

Chi Chi 25

Vodka Collins 26

Moscow Mule 27

Blue Hawaii 28

Watermelon Cooler 29

Rosemary Baby 30

Minty Vodka Lemonade 31

TEQUILA 32

All the King's Men 32

Santa Carla 33

Cinnamon-Tamarind Margarita 34

Paloma Brava 35

Mexican Vampires 36

Siesta 37

Matador 38

Chimayo 38

Ruirita 39

GIN 41

Honolulu Gin Cocktail 41

The Obituary Cocktail 42

Auld Draper 43

Martini 43

Moon River 44

London Fog Cocktail 45

Bloodhound 46

Pamplemousse 47

Old Etonian 48

WHISKEY 49

Evening Shade.. 49

Old Pal.. 50

Scarlet Starlet 51

New York Cocktail.. 52

Melisse Whiskey Sour 53

Bordeaux Sour 54

The Good Doctor 55

White Whiskey Punch....................................... 55

Algonquin Cocktail... 56

Crownberry Apple.. 57

MOCKTAILS 58

Millionaire Sour 58

Arizona Sunset 59

Passion Fruit Summer Drink 60

Asian Pear Sparkler.. 61

Cucumber Mojito... 62

Rosemary Cranberry Refresher 63

Sangria 64

Roy Rodgers 65

Non-alcoholic Margaritas 65

Moscow Mule Mocktail 67

The Palauxma 67

BAR SNACKS 69

   Roasted Chickpeas 69

   Date Almond Balls 70

   Baked Sweet Potato Chips 71

   Almond Vanilla Snack Bars 72

   Nutella Brownies 73

   Pineapple Ice 74

   Frozen Yogurt Blueberries 74

   Peanut Butter Banana Ice Cream 75

   Spicy Popcorn 76

INTRODUCTION

Summer is all about clear blue skies, bright sunny days, soothing gentle breeze and birds chirping happily. But it's definitely incomplete without a chilled glass of great tasting and invigorating cocktail in hand. Yes, cocktails are what make a fantastic summer. Whether you're planning a party or just by yourself at the beach, in your courtyard, by the pool side, at the park or garden, there is no better way to complement the weather than to indulge yourself in these refreshing treats. And even after summer, these delicious revitalizing cocktails are sure to provide the desired maximum satisfaction anytime of the day.

What's more! You don't need to visit the cocktail lounge every time you need to cool off with one. You can make the finest delicious cocktails at home or anywhere you find yourself. Mixing your own cocktail is not as hard as it looks. Once you know the right ingredients, measurements, tools and the right glassware for your favorite cocktails, you are not far from becoming a pro.

This is what this book will do for you, as it's a compilation of fantastic cocktail recipes for the summer and beyond. Each of these recipes comes with a unique taste that is made just for you. Additionally, it includes some bar snacks to go along with the drinks and to keep you fuller for longer.

The recipes have been split into eight categories based on different beverage types. Therefore, you are sure to find some cocktails made with your preferred drink. For vodka lovers, cool-off with some Ice Blue Martini, Watermelon Coolant or a Vodka Collins. For Tiki fans, come alive with a cool glass of Zombie, sail off with The Ancient Mariner or enjoy the delicious sting of the Scorpion. Non-alcoholics are not let out of this fun. You can try our Cucumber Mojitos, Sangria, or slowly enjoy the Arizona Sunset...and feel refreshed!

Types Of Cocktail Glasses

To create a great drinking experience, you need the right choice of glassware to serve your cocktails. For instance, you get this feeling of sophistication and class when drinking a martini from a martini glass and the Moscow mule doesn't seem to taste right without the mug that's made specifically for it. Using the correct glassware for your cocktail also helps improve the aroma and maintain the right temperature of the drink.

Here are the major glass cups you'll be needing to serve your cocktails:

Traditional Cocktail cup: this looks like an inverted glass cone on a long narrow glass rod. They usually measure from 3-6 ounces of drink. The wide rim allows the drinker to first enjoy the aroma oozing from drink before tasting the drink itself.

Highball Glass: a long flat-bottomed tumbler used to serve tall cocktails over ice. It's also used for carbonated cocktails with low alcohol content.

The Collins Glass: can be said to be a variation of the highball glass with a wider rim and shorter height.

Lowball Glass: also called rocks glass (because it's used to serve drinks "on the rocks") is mainly used for spirits and highly alcoholic cocktails. It has a thicker base and can accommodate large ice-cube chunks. This short tumbler can contain about 6-8 ounces of drink (i.e. without the ice though).

The Coupe: looks like a shallow bowl on a narrow stem and is great for drinks without ice. It's mostly used for Martinis, Daiquiris, Manhattans or Sidecars.

Hurricane Glass: derives its name from the hurricane lamp-like glass cups used to serve the hurricane cocktail in the 1940s. Today, the hurricane glass is also used for Pina Coladas.

Martini Glass: as the name implies are specifically used for martinis. They have a wider rim than the classic cocktail glass with a conical base.

Margarita Glass: differs slightly from the cocktail glass and is specially used to serve Margaritas (even though many persons have adopted other glassware to serve this sophisticated drink).

Nick And Nora Glasses: which are actually smaller martini glasses.

Tiki Mugs: makes drinking Tiki cocktails fun.

Moscow Mule Mug: Copper mugs for Moscow mules.

Julep Cup: used to serve mint julep and sometimes fruits and ice cream

Cocktail Bar Utensils

If you are going to be mixing great cocktails this summer, you'll need the right tools and utensils. Here are a few necessary equipments you'll need to kit up your cocktail bar.

Cocktail Shakers: there are two general types– the Boston and the cobbler shakers. The **Boston Shaker** consist of a metal canister over a pint glass and is often used by professional bar tenders. **The Traditional/ Cobbler Shaker** on the other hand, looks more like a bottle consisting of a metal or glass container, topped with an inbuilt strainer and a cover. This is more commonly used to mix drinks.

Hawthorne Strainer: a multipurpose strainer with a semi circular spring that helps the device fit tightly to a shaker. It gets rid of unwanted particles from your drink.

Measuring Jigger: you'll need this to measure out your drinks accurately. Get one with a good pour spout.

Ice Kit: a small ice-making making is essential and faster than freezing water in ice-block molds.

Bar Spoon: a "heavy" long- handled stainless steel spoon with a hammer-like end for muddling herbs. The spoon can also be used to measure out small quantities of ingredients.

Muddler: get a wooden muddler if you don't already have a tool that can do the job, like the one that comes with an ice kit.

Citrus Juicer: for squeezing out juice from mostly citrus fruits. There are different kinds out there but look out for one with a reaming cone, strainer and a spout.

Peeler: you'll need this when garnishing your drink with a citrus peel. For a thinner and fancier spiral twist, use a channel knife.

Mixing Glass: if u don't already have a Boston shaker (as one part of it is already a mixing glass).

Julep Strainer: if you are using a mixing glass, I bet this will come in handy.

Fine Mesh Strainer: for drinks that require double straining. You use this after using the Hawthorne or julep strainer.

You'll also be needing some bitters (I recommend Peychaud's, Angostura and any orange bitter), simple syrup, coarse salt (to rim cocktail glasses) and club sodas or tonics.

So now that you're properly equipped with the right tools and glassware for a wonderful cocktail treat, let's get mixing some of these refreshing delights.

CLASSIC TIKI

Mai Tai

Whenever you are in the tropics, this should be a worthy companion.

Preparation time: 5 minutes

Cooking time: 0 minute

Servings: 1

Ingredients:

2 ounces of Jamaican rum

½ ounce of Curacao

¼ ounce of rock-candy syrup

¼ ounce of orgeat

1 medium lime, juiced

To garnish, mint

Directions:

1. In a cocktail shaker, pour in all the ingredients and fill it with ice.

2. Shake thoroughly for 10 seconds. Fill a double old-fashioned glass with crushed ice and strain the drink into it.

3. Garnish with lime shell and mint.

Fog Cutter

A favorite among true tiki fans.

Preparation time: 5 minutes

Cooking time: 0 minute

Servings: 1

Ingredients:

2 ounces of orange juice, freshly squeezed

1½ ounces of white rum

1 ounce of lemon juice, freshly squeezed

½ ounce of brandy

½ ounce of orgeat

½ ounce of Amontillado sherry

½ ounce of gin

Directions:

1. In a cocktail shaker, pour in all the ingredients except the sherry and fill it with ice.

2. Shake thoroughly. Fill a highball glass with ice and pour the drink into it carefully.

3. Garnish with a sprig of mint.

Rum Swizzle

A delicious cocktail that is easy to make.

Preparation time: 5 minutes

Cooking time: 0 minute

Servings: 1

Ingredients:

2 ounces of grapefruit juice

2 ounces of amber rhum agricole

½ ounce of brown sugar simple syrup

1/8 ounce of grenadine

7 large mint leaves

Crushed ice

Directions:

1. Muddle the mint leaves in a Collins glass before adding the rest of the ingredients.

2. Combine by spinning a long bar spoon between your palms or using a swizzle.

3. Use the crushed ice as toppings.

Painkiller

A unique twist to the pina colada.

Preparation time: 10 minutes

Cooking time: 0 minute

Servings: 1-2

Ingredients:

4 ounces of pineapple juice

2 ounces of dark or navy rum

1 ounce of orange juice

1 ounce cream of coconut

For garnish, grated nutmeg

Directions:

1. In a cocktail shaker, pour in all the ingredients and fill it with ice.

2. Shake thoroughly. Fill a highball glass with fresh ice and strain the drink into it.

3. Top with grated nutmeg.

Scorpion

Add a bit of delicious sting to your cocktail.

Preparation time: 5 minutes

Cooking time: 0 minute

Servings: 1

Ingredients:

1 cup of crushed ice

2 ounces of light Puerto Rican rum

2 ounces of orange juice, freshly squeezed

1½ ounce of lemon juice, freshly squeezed

1 ounce of brandy

½ ounce of orgeat syrup

Directions:

1. Blend the ingredients together in a blender for 10 seconds.

2. Pour the unstrained drink into a wide brandy snifter or double old fashioned glass.

3. Top with your preferred garnish.

Planters Punch

Customize this recipe however way you want.

Preparation time: 10 minutes

Cooking time: 0 minute

Servings: 4-6

Ingredients:

1 cup of rum

1 cup of orange juice

1 cup of pineapple juice

¼ cup of grenadine

¼ cup of Southern Comfort

¼ cup of almond liqueur

Juice of 3 limes

Cherries, for garnish

Pineapple slice, for garnish

Lime slice, for garnish

Directions:

1. In a pitcher, combine the rum, orange juice, pineapple juice, grenadine, Southern Comfort, almond liqueur and lime juice. Fill with ice cubes.

2. Fill the drinking glasses with ice cubes, pour in the drink and garnish.

Zombie

A fun and delicious combo of rum and fruit juice.

Preparation time: 5 minutes

Cooking time: 0 minute

Servings: 1

Ingredients:

2 ounces of orange juice

1 ounce of apricot liquor

1 ounce of Bacardi 151 Rum

1 ounce of dark rum

1 ounce of light rum

A dash of lime bitters

A handful of ice

An orange slice, for garnish

Cherry, for garnish

Directions:

1. In a cocktail shaker, mix together the orange juice, apricot liquor, dark rum, light rum and bitters.

2. Fill a large glass with ice, pour the drink into it and top with the Bacardi 151 rum.

3. Use the orange slice and cherry as garnish.

The Saturn

The cocktail every summer party should have.

Preparation time: 5 minutes

Cooking time: 0 minute

Servings: 1

Ingredients:

1¼ ounces of gin

½ ounce of passion fruit syrup

½ ounce of lemon juice

¼ ounce of falernum

¼ ounce of orgeat syrup

Directions:

1. Put all the ingredients in a blender and blend with crushed ice.

2. Pour into a tall glass and garnish with mint sprig or pineapple wedge.

The Ancient Mariner

A refreshing tiki classic.

Preparation time: 2 minutes

Cooking time: 0 minute

Servings: 1

Ingredients:

1 ounce of dark Jamaican rum

1 ounce of demerara rum

½ ounce of simple syrup

½ ounce of grapefruit juice, freshly squeezed

¼ ounce of allspice dram

¾ ounce of lime juice, freshly squeezed

Crushed ice

Lime wedge

Mint sprig

Directions:

1. Add the rums, syrup, grapefruit juice, allspice dram and lime juice to a double old-fashioned glass with crushed ice. Gently stir.

2. Garnish with the lime wedge and mint sprig.

RUM

Cranberry Zombie
A unique twist to the zombie cocktail.

Preparation time: 5 minutes

Cooking time: 0 minute

Servings: 1

Ingredients:

1 ounce of dark rum

1 ounce of lime juice

½ ounce of Bacardi 151

½ ounce of white rum

½ ounce of golden rum

2 teaspoon of cranberry juice

1 teaspoon of sugar

Directions:

1. In a cocktail shaker, pour all the ingredients except the Bacardi 151.

2. Shake well and pour into an ice-filled tall glass.

3. Gently spoon the Bacardi over the drink for it to float on top.

4. Garnish with a cherry or cranberry.

Pina Colada

A favorite among beach party goers.

Preparation time: 5 minutes

Cooking time: 0 minute

Servings: 2

Ingredients:

4 ounces of cream of coconut

4 ounces of pineapple juice

3 ounces of light rum

2 cups of crushed ice

Fresh nutmeg

Directions:

1. Blend the cream of coconut, pineapple juice, rum and ice in a blender until it is smooth.

2. Pour the drink into a glass and sprinkle with nutmeg.

3. Garnish with a slice of pineapple or orange.

Mojito

No party is complete without this famous cocktail.

Preparation time: 3 minutes

Cooking time: 0 minute

Servings: 2

Ingredients:

1½ ounces of Bacardi superior rum

12 mint leaves

2 tablespoons of simple syrup

½ lime

Club soda

Directions:

1. Muddle the mint leaves with the lime. Cover it with the simple syrup and add ice as topping.

2. Add the rum and top with the soda. Combine thoroughly.

3. Garnish with a sprig of mint and lime wedge.

Strawberry Daiquiri

This fruit and rum combo is sure to be a crowd pleaser.

Preparation time: 5 minutes

Cooking time: 0 minute

Servings: 2

Ingredients:

4 ounces of light rum

½ cup of frozen strawberries

½ cup of fresh strawberries

1 lime, juiced

For garnish: 1 cup of ice sliced lime

Directions:

1. Blend the rum, strawberries and lime juice in a blender until it is smooth.

2. Pour into glasses and garnish with the sliced lime.

Caribbean Rum Punch

Simply yummy and amazing.

Preparation time: 5 minutes

Cooking time: 0 minute

Servings: 2

Ingredients:

4 ounces of pineapple juice

4 ounces of orange juice

1½ ounces of light rum

1½ ounces of dark rum

½ ounce of lime juice

A dash of grenadine

Directions:

1. Combine all the ingredients together and pour over ice.

2. Sprinkle nutmeg on top and garnish with a cherry and orange slice.

Bushwacker

A potent milkshake.

Preparation time: 5 minutes

Cooking time: 0 minute

Servings: 3

Ingredients:

2 ounces of amaretto

2 ounces of bailey

2 ounces of cream of coconut

2 ounces of coconut rum

2 ounces of kahlua

2 ounces of vodka

A pinch of nutmeg

Chocolate syrup

Directions:

1. In a glass, drizzle chocolate syrup.

2. Blend the remaining ingredients, except the nutmeg with ice in a blender and pour into the glass.

3. Sprinkle with the nutmeg.

Hurricane

Fruity, delicious and iconic.

Preparation time: 5 minutes

Cooking time: 0 minute

Servings: 2

Ingredients:

6 ounces of orange juice

6 ounces of passion fruit juice

3 ounces of dark rum

2 ounces of light rum

2 tablespoons of grenadine

2 maraschino cherries

2 orange slices

Directions:

1. Combine the rums, orange juice, passion fruit juice and grenadine in a large liquid measuring cup.

2. Pour this mix over a glass filled with ice.

3. Garnish with the maraschino cherry and orange slice.

Dirty Banana

A drink that will transport you to the beach.

Preparation time: 5 minutes

Cooking time: 0 minute

Servings: 2

Ingredients:

4 ounces of milk

2 ounces of rum cream liqueur

2 ounces of dark rum

2 ounces of Tia Maria

1 ounce of simple syrup

Ice

¾ banana

Directions:

1. Blend all the ingredients until it is thick and smooth.

2. Pour the creamy mix into glasses.

3. Sprinkle with nutmeg, cinnamon or allspice.

Rum Sunset

Easy to make and absolutely potent.

Preparation time: 5 minutes

Cooking time: 0 minute

Servings: 2

Ingredients:

3 ounces of light rum

12 ounces of orange juice

2 tablespoons of grenadine

Lime slices, garnish

Directions:

1. Mix the rum and orange juice together. Keep 1/3 of the mixture aside.

2. Pour 2/3 of the mixture into two glasses filled with ice. Keep aside.

3. Mix the reserved 1/3 rum mixture with the grenadine and pour it into the glasses slowly.

4. Garnish with the slices of lime.

VODKA

Bloody Mary

The perfect breakfast and hangover cure.

Preparation time: 5 minutes

Cooking time: 0 minute

Servings: 1

Ingredients:

1 cup of ice cubes

¼ cup of tomato juice

3 tablespoons of vodka

1 teaspoon of Worcestershire sauce

¼ teaspoon of fresh lemon juice

¾ teaspoon of horseradish, freshly grated

3 dashes of hot pepper sauce

1 celery stalk

A dash of freshly ground black pepper

A pinch of salt

1 lemon wedge, optional

Directions:

1. Mix the tomato juice, Worcestershire sauce, vodka, hot sauce, pepper, salt and horseradish in an 11-ounce highball glass.

2. Fill a second glass with ice and pour the tomato juice mixture into the ice-filled glass. Mix well by pouring the mixture back and forth for about 3 to 4 times.

3. Sprinkle lemon juice over it and garnish with the lemon wedge and celery stalk.

Ice Blue Martini

Create this masterpiece with just 3 ingredients.

Preparation time: 5 minutes

Cooking time: 0 minute

Servings: 1

Ingredients:

3 ounces of lemonade

2 ounces of hpnotiq liqueur

½ ounce of vodka

Directions:

1. Combine all the ingredients together and shake with ice.

2. Strain the mixture into a martini glass.

3. Garnish with a lemon twist.

Chi Chi

This fruity drink will have you doing the cha-cha in no time.

Preparation time: 7 minutes

Cooking time: 0 minute

Servings: 2

Ingredients:

4 ounces of pineapple juice

3 ounces of vodka

2 ounces of cream of coconut

1 cup of crushed ice

1 teaspoon of confectioners' sugar

2 maraschino cherries, on toothpicks (garnish)

2 pineapple slices (garnish)

Directions:

1. Blend all the ingredients except the pineapple and cherries in a blender on high speed for about 30 seconds until it is smooth and frothy.

2. Pour into two chilled Collins glass.

3. Garnish with the cherry and pineapple slices.

Vodka Collins

A fizzy and lemony drink that is great for parties.

Preparation time: 2 minutes

Cooking time: 0 minute

Servings: 1

Ingredients:

2 ounces of vodka

2/3 ounces of fresh lemon juice

2/3 ounces of simple sugar syrup

Club soda

2 cherries with stem ice cubes

2 lemon wheels, cut into halves

Directions:

1. Fill a mixing glass with ice, pour in the vodka, lemon juice and syrup. Shake well.

2. Strain the mixture and pour into a serving glass filled with ice.

3. Drop one half of the lemon wheels into the glass and top with soda. Stir gently.

4. Use the remaining lemon wheel and cherry to garnish. Add straw and serve.

Moscow Mule

A favorite with vodka-lovers.

Preparation time: 3 minutes

Cooking time: 0 minute

Servings: 1

Ingredients:

3 ounces of ginger beer

2 ounces of vodka

½ a lime, juiced

Lime wheel, juiced

Directions:

1. Pour all the ingredients to an ice-filled highball glass or Moscow mule mug.

2. Use the lime wheel to garnish.

Blue Hawaii

Has a fun color with a soothing taste.

Preparation time: 8 minutes

Cooking time:

Servings: 1

Ingredients:

2 ounces of Blue Curacao

2 ounces of unsweetened pineapple juice

1½ ounces of sour mix

1½ ounces of vodka

½ ounce of half & half

Pineapple wedge, for garnish

Maraschino cherry, (optional), for garnish

Orchid (optional), for garnish

Directions:

1. In a cocktail shaker, mix the Curacao, pineapple juice, sour mix, vodka and half & half.

2. Pour this mix into a hurricane glass filled with crushed ice.

3. Garnish with the pineapple wedge, cherry and orchid.

Watermelon Cooler

An easy and refreshing drink.

Preparation time: 5 minutes

Cooking time: 0 minute

Servings: 8

Ingredients:

3 pounds of watermelon

1¼ cups of ginger ale

¼ cup of vodka

2 tablespoons of fresh mint

1 tablespoon of fresh lemon juice

1 tablespoon of superfine sugar

3-4 splashes of bitters

Ice cubes

For garnish, fresh mint

Directions:

1. In a food processor, puree the watermelon.

2. Muddle the 2 tablespoons of mint in a large pitcher with sugar. Fill the pitcher with ice cubes.

3. Pour in the pureed watermelon, vodka, ginger ale, bitters and lemon juice.

4. Use the fresh mint as garnish.

Rosemary Baby

A drink based on the classic film.

Preparation time: 5 minutes

Cooking time: 0 minute

Servings: 1

Ingredients:

2½ ounces vodka

½ ounce fresh lime juice

A dash of grenadine

For garnish: rosemary sprigs

Directions:

1. Add the vodka, lime juice and grenadine to a shaker filled with ice.

2. Strain the mixture into a champagne glass.

3. Garnish with the rosemary sprig.

Minty Vodka Lemonade

Perfect for a hot day at the beach.

Preparation time: 15 minutes

Cooking time: 0 minute

Servings: 8-10

Ingredients:

8-16 ounces of vodka

8 cups of cold water

½ - ¾ cup of sugar or honey

Mint leaves from 1 medium bunch

4 lemons or limes, quartered and seeded

Ice cubes

For garnish: lemon or lime slices

Directions:

1. Blend the quartered lemons or limes with 2 cups of water, some ice, sugar or honey and half of the mint leaves until it is a bit foamy with a whitish color.

2. Strain this mixture and add the remaining water.

3. Pour in the vodka and serve with ice.

4. Garnish with the lime slices and remaining mint leaves.

TEQUILA

All the King's Men
Celebrate Cinco de Mayo with this smooth cocktail.

Preparation time: 2 minutes

Cooking time: 0 minute

Servings: 1

Ingredients:

1½ ounces of reposado tequila

1 ounce of lemon juice, freshly squeezed

1-2 ounces of ginger beer

½ ounce of ruby port

½ ounce of Averna

½ teaspoon of honey

2 blackberries, optional

1 paper-thin slice fresh ginger

Directions:

1. Fill a cocktail shaker with ice and pour in all the ingredients except the ginger ale, blackberries and ginger slices. Cover and shake thoroughly for 15 seconds until it is chilled.

2. Strain the mixture into an ice-filled Collins glass wile pouring in the ginger ale at the same time.

3. Garnish with the blackberries and ginger slices.

Santa Carla

One of the famous tequila cocktails available.

Preparation time: 10 minutes

Cooking time: 0 minute

Servings: 1

Ingredients:

2 ounces of silver tequila

¾ ounce of simple syrup

1 ounce of fresh lemon juice

Sparkling water

3 dashes of grapefruit bitters

For garnish, mint sprig

For garnish, lemon wheel

Directions:

1. Add the tequila, syrup, lemon juice and grapefruit bitters to an ice-filled Collins glass.

2. Top with the sparkling water and gently stir.

3. Garnish with the mint sprig and lemon wheel.

Cinnamon-Tamarind Margarita

Refreshing, tart, and tasty.

Preparation time: 10 minutes

Cooking time: 0 minute

Servings: 1

Ingredients:

Cocktail:

2 ounces of blanco or reposado tequila

1¼ ounce of lime juice, freshly squeezed

½ ounce of lemon juice, freshly squeezed

½ ounce of simple syrup

¼ ounce of Cointreau

¾ ounce of tamarind concentrate

Ice

For garnish, cinnamon stick (optional)

Rim:

2 tablespoons of lime juice, freshly squeezed

1 teaspoon of kosher salt

1 teaspoon of sugar

½ teaspoon of ground cinnamon

½ teaspoon of cayenne

Directions:

1. In a small bowl, combine the salt, cayenne, sugar and cinnamon. Pour this mixture on a saucer.

2. Get another saucer and pour 2 tablespoons of lime juice on it. Coat the outer rim of your serving glass by turning it in the lime juice. Slowly spin this glass in the cinnamon mixture in order to coat.

3. In an ice-filled mixing glass, add the tequila, lemon juice, lime juice, syrup, Cointreau and tamarind concentrate. Shake thoroughly for about 30 seconds.

4. Strain the drink into the serving glass and garnish with the cinnamon stick, if preferred.

Paloma Brava

A forever classic!

Preparation time: 5 minutes

Cooking time: 0 minute

Servings: 1

Ingredients:

6 ounces of fresh grapefruit juice

4 ounces of grapefruit soda

2 ounces of fresh orange juice

1½ ounces of reposado tequila

¾ ounce of fresh lime juice

Agave nectar

A pinch of salt

For garnish, lime wheel

Directions:

1. Pour in the grapefruit juice, orange juice, tequila, lime juice and salt into an ice-filled large glass mug. Gently stir.

2. Top with the grapefruit soda and add the agave nectar.

3. Garnish with the lime wheel.

Mexican Vampires
The original Mexican cocktail.

Preparation time: 5 minutes

Cooking time: 0 minute

Servings: 1

Ingredients:

3 ounces of Sangrita

1½ ounces of citrus-flavored soda

1½ fluid ounces of silver tequila (100% agave)

Juice of ½ lime

A pinch of Mexican-style chili powder with lime

Ice cubes

Directions:

1. Pour the Sangrita, soda, tequila, lime juice and fruit seasoning powder into an ice-filled highball glass. Stir to combine thoroughly.

Siesta

Indulge your senses in this luxurious drink.

Preparation time: 10 minutes

Cooking time: 0 minute

Servings: 1

Ingredients:

2 ounces of silver tequila (100% agave)

½ ounce of simple syrup

½ ounce of campari

½ ounce of grapefruit juice, freshly squeezed

½ ounce of lime juice, freshly squeezed

To garnish, grapefruit twist

Directions:

1. Pour the tequila, syrup, campari, lime juice and grapefruit juice into an ice-filled cocktail shaker. Shake thoroughly.

2. Strain the drink into a chilled coupe.

3. Garnish drink with the grapefruit twist.

Matador

A delicious variation of the margarita.

Preparation time: 5 minutes

Cooking time: 0 minute

Servings: 1

Ingredients:

1½ ounces of blanco tequila

1/3 ounce of fresh lime juice

1 ounce of unsweetened pineapple juice

Ice

Directions:

1. Pour the tequila, lime juice and pineapple juice into an ice-filled cocktail shaker. Shake thoroughly.

2. Strain the drink into a rocks glass filled with ice.

Chimayo

Complex-tasting and a classic from the town of Chimayo.

Preparation time: 15 minutes

Cooking time: 0 minute

Servings: 8

Ingredients:

2 cups of unsweetened apple juice or apple cider

1 cup of tequila, preferably gold

¼ cup of fresh lemon juice

¼ cup of crème de cassis

Ice cube

For garnish, apple slices, unpeeled,

Directions:

1. Combine the apple juice or cider, tequila, lemon juice and crème de cassis in a pitcher.

2. Pour the mix into glasses filled halfway with ice.

3. Garnish each glass with an apple slice.

Ruirita

This drink is only for the brave.

Preparation time: 5 minutes

Cooking time: 0 minute

Servings: 1

Ingredients:

2 ounces of tequila blanco (100% agave)

½ ounce of lime juice

½ ounce of Cynar

¼ ounce of simple syrup

3 dashes of rhubarb bitters

2 drops of orange flower water

Ice

Directions:

1. Fill a mixing glass with ice and add the tequila, lime juice, cynar, bitters and syrup. Shake thoroughly.

2. Use the orange flower water to rinse a chilled serving glass. Strain the cocktail into the glass and serve.

GIN

Honolulu Gin Cocktail

Ever since its creation in 1930, this drink has remained a classic.

Preparation time: 10 minutes

Cooking time: 0 minute

Servings: 1

Ingredients:

2 ounces of gin

½ ounce of orange juice

½ ounce of pineapple juice

¼ ounce of simple syrup

¼ ounce of lemon juice

A dash of Angostura bitters

For garnish, lemon spiral

Super-fine sugar, to rim (optional)

Directions:

1. If you desire, rim a cocktail glass with sugar.

2. Fill a chilled cocktail shaker with ice and pour the remaining ingredients. Shake thoroughly.

3. Strain the drink into the prepared cocktail glass and garnish with the lemon spiral.

The Obituary Cocktail

Put things to rest with this smooth drink.

Preparation time: 5 minutes

Cooking time: 0 minute

Servings: 1

Ingredients:

2 ounces of gin

¾ ounce of absinthe

¾ ounce of dry vermouth

Directions:

1. In a cocktail shaker containing cracked ice, mix all the ingredients together and stir.

2. Strain drink into a chilled cocktail glass and garnish as desired.

Auld Draper

Simple to prepare and rich in flavors.

Preparation time: 5 minutes

Cooking time: 0 minute

Servings: 1

Ingredients:

2 ounces of dry gin

3 dashes of orange bitters

¾ ounce of byrrh

Flamed orange peel, to garnish

Directions:

1. Pour the gin, bitters and byrrh into a mixing glass filled 2/3 with ice. Stir for about 20 seconds until it is well-chilled.

2. Strain drink into a fresh ice-filled rocks glass.

3. Garnish with the orange peel.

Martini

No party is complete without this forever classic.

Preparation time: 5 minutes

Cooking time: 0 minute

Servings: 1

Ingredients:

1 ounce of dry vermouth

2 ounces of dry gin

Dash of orange bitters

Directions:

1. Mix all the ingredients in an ice-filled mixing glass. Thoroughly stir to chill.

2. Strain drink into a chilled cocktail glass.

Moon River
A delicious recipe that will leave you wanting more.

Preparation time: 5 minutes

Cooking time: 0 minute

Servings: 1

Ingredients:

1 ounce of apricot brandy

1 ounce of gin

½ ounce of lemon juice

½ ounce of Galliano

3/4 ounce of cointreau

Maraschino cherry, to garnish

Directions:

1. Mix all the ingredients except the cherry in an ice-filled cocktail shaker. Thoroughly stir to chill.

2. Strain drink into a chilled cocktail glass.

3. Garnish with the cherry.

London Fog Cocktail
Mix and serve chilled.

Preparation time: 5 minutes

Cooking time: 0 minute

Servings: 1

Ingredients:

¼ ounce of pernod

1½ ounces of London dry gin

Directions:

1. Mix all the ingredients in an ice-filled cocktail shaker. Thoroughly stir for 30 seconds to chill.

2. Strain drink into a chilled martini glass.

Bloodhound

Very simple to make and refreshingly tasty.

Preparation time: 5 minutes

Cooking time: 0 minute

Servings: 1

Ingredients:

1 ounce of gin

½ ounce of strawberry liqueur

½ ounce of sweet vermouth

½ ounce of dry vermouth

Fresh strawberry, to garnish

Directions:

1. Mix all the ingredients except the strawberry in an ice-filled cocktail shaker. Thoroughly shake to chill for 30 seconds.

2. Strain drink into a chilled cocktail glass.

3. Garnish with the strawberry.

Pamplemousse

Light and refreshing.

Preparation time: 5 minutes

Cooking time: 0 minute

Servings: 1

Ingredients:

1 ounce gin

1 ounce of white grapefruit juice, freshly squeezed

½ ounce of elderflower liqueur, such as St. Germain

½ ounce of lemon juice, freshly squeezed

For garnish, basil leaf

Directions:

1. Mix all the ingredients except the basil leaf, in an ice-filled cocktail shaker. Thoroughly shake for 30 seconds to chill.

2. Strain drink into a chilled cocktail glass.

3. Garnish with the basil leaf.

Old Etonian

A gin cocktail named after the alumni of Eton College.

Preparation time: 5 minutes

Cooking time: 0 minute

Servings: 1

Ingredients:

1½ ounces of gin

1½ ounces of Lillet Blanc

2 orange bitters

A dash of amaretto

Directions:

1. Mix all the ingredients in an ice-filled cocktail shaker. Thoroughly shake for 10-15 seconds to chill.

2. Strain drink into a chilled cocktail glass.

WHISKEY

Evening Shade
A fruity whiskey combo.

Preparation time: 5 minutes

Cooking time: 0 minute

Servings: 1

Ingredients:

2 ounces of peach purée

1½ ounces of corn whiskey

½ ounce of lime juice

½ ounce of pomegranate liqueur

¾ ounce of ginger liqueur

3 cucumber slices

2 sprigs of lemon balm

Directions:

1. In a cocktail shaker, muddle cucumber slices with the lime juice.

2. Add the whiskey, peach pure, pomegranate liqueur, ginger liqueur and ice. Shake thoroughly.

3. Fill a Collins glass with cracked ice and strain the drink into it.

4. Garnish drink with lemon balm.

Old Pal

A cousin of the classic Negroni.

Preparation time: 3 minutes

Cooking time: 0 minute

Servings: 1

Ingredients:

2 ounces of rye whiskey

1 ounce of dry vermouth

1 ounce of campari

For garnish, lemon twist

Directions:

1. In a shaker filled with ice, add the whiskey, vermouth and campari.

2. Strain the mix into a chilled cocktail glass.

3. Garnish with the lemon twist.

Scarlet Starlet

This well-balanced blend is perfect for warm weather.

Preparation time: 7 minutes

Cooking time: 0 minute

Servings: 1

Ingredients:

1½ ounces of Scotch whisky

½ ounce of hibiscus syrup

½ ounce of vanilla cognac liqueur

½ ounce of strawberry syrup

¾ ounce of egg white, lightly beaten

¾ ounce of fresh lime juice

1 organic red rose petal

Directions:

1. In a cocktail shaker, mix the whiskey, hibiscus syrup, liqueur, strawberry syrup, lime juice and egg white. Shake until it is frothy.

2. Add ice and shake well to chill.

3. Strain into a chilled champagne coupe.

4. Garnish with the red rose petal.

New York Cocktail

Strictly for the most committed whiskey lovers.

Preparation time: 5 minutes

Cooking time: 0 minute

Servings: 1

Ingredients:

1½ ounces of rye whiskey

¼ teaspoon of grenadine

½ ounce of fresh lime juice

½ teaspoon of confectioners' sugar

Orange peel, to garnish

Directions:

1. Add the rye whiskey, grenadine, lime juice and sugar to a shaker filled with a cup of ice. Cover and shake thoroughly for about 10-15 seconds.

2. Strain into a chilled cocktail glass.

3. Garnish with orange peel.

Melisse Whiskey Sour

The ladies will love this.

Preparation time: 10 minutes

Cooking time: 0 minute

Servings: 1

Ingredients:

2 ounces of bourbon

Angostura bitters

¾ ounce of simple syrup

1 ounce of fresh lemon juice

1 white of large egg

Directions:

1. In a stainless steel shaker, pour in the bourbon, syrup, lemon juice and egg white with a big block of ice. Shake thoroughly.

2. Strain the mixture into a chilled cocktail glass. Tap the bottom of the glass to remove air bubbles.

3. Garnish with four drops of bitters once foam appears on top.

Bordeaux Sour

A perfect balance of tart and sweet.

Preparation time: 10 minutes

Cooking time: 0 minute

Servings: 1

Ingredients:

2 ounces of whiskey

1 ounce of seltzer

1 ounce of lemon juice

1 ounce of Lillet Rouge

5 dashes of orange bitters

1 egg white

1 tablespoon of maple syrup

2 maraschino cherries, garnish

Directions:

1. In a cocktail shaker, muddle the syrup, lemon juice and cherries together.

2. Pour in the whiskey, egg white, Lillet Rouge, bitter and ice. Shake thoroughly.

3. Strain into an ice-filled old fashioned glass.

4. Add the seltzer as toppings and garnish with cherry.

The Good Doctor

A drink that lives up to its name.

Preparation time: 5 minutes

Cooking time: 0 minute

Servings: 1

Ingredients:

6 ounces of Dr. Pepper

1½ ounces of rye whiskey

1½ ounces of amaro

Orange slice, to garnish

Directions:

1. Pour the whiskey and amaro into an ice-filled glass. Top with the Dr. Pepper.

2. Squeeze the slice of orange into the mix and garnish the drink with the slice.

White Whiskey Punch

Transform this winter drink into a drink for warm weather.

Preparation time: 5 minutes

Cooking time: 0 minute

Servings: 1

Ingredients:

2 ounces of fresh pineapple juice

2 ounces of white whiskey

1 ounce of simple syrup

1 ounce of fresh lime juice

Pineapple wedge, garnish

Directions:

1. In an ice-filled shaker, combine the pineapple juice, whiskey, syrup and lime juice. Shake thoroughly.

2. Strain the drink into an ice-filled rocks glass and garnish with the pineapple wedge.

Algonquin Cocktail
Beat the heat with this potent mix.

Preparation time: 5 minutes

Cooking time: 0 minute

Servings:1

Ingredients:

1½ ounces of rye whiskey

¾ ounce of pineapple juice

¾ ounce of dry vermouth

Directions:

1. Add all the ingredients to a cocktail shaker containing ice cubes. Shake thoroughly.

2. Strain drink into a chilled cocktail glass.

Crownberry Apple
Requires no effort at all.

Preparation time: 5 minutes

Cooking time: 0 minute

Servings: 1

Ingredients:

4 ounces of cranberry juice

½ ounce of apple whisky

1 crown royal regal

Directions:

1. Pour the apple whiskey into a rocks glass containing ice.

2. Top the drink with the cranberry juice. Gently stir.

3. Garnish with an apple wheel.

MOCKTAILS

Millionaire Sour

For those times when you are feeling fancy.

Preparation time: 5 minutes

Cooking time: 0 minute

Servings: 1

Ingredients:

2 ounces of ginger ale

2 ounces of lemon simple syrup

¼ shot of grenadine

¼ cup of crushed ice

Lemon slice, garnish

Cherry, to garnish

Directions:

1. Pour all ingredients except garnish into ice filled glass.

2. Garnish with the lemon slice and cherry.

Arizona Sunset

Beautiful to look at, refreshing to drink.

Preparation time: 5 minutes

Cooking time: 0 minute

Servings: 2

Ingredients:

1 cup of orange juice

1 cup of Sprite soft drink

Grenadine

Ice

Maraschino cherries, garnish (optional)

Directions:

1. Put the ice in 2 glasses and add a splash of grenadine to each of the glass.

2. Combine the sprite and orange juice in a small pitcher. Pour this mixture over the grenadine in the glasses slowly.

3. Garnish with the cherries.

Passion Fruit Summer Drink

Bright, colorful and excellent.

Preparation time: 10 minutes

Cooking time: 0 minute

Servings: 4

Ingredients:

8 passion fruits

1 cup of sparkling soda

½ cup of mint leaves

Juice of 4 oranges

3 inches of fresh ginger, cut into thin sticks

2 limes, cut into ½-inch-pieces

Ice cubes

Directions:

1. In a bowl, muddle the pieces of lime, mint leaves and half of the ginger sticks. Pour this mixture into a pitcher.

2. Divide the passion fruits in half and scoop out its flesh, add to the pitcher. Pour in the orange juice and ice cubes. Stir.

3. Top the drink with the soda, a mint leaf and some ginger sticks.

Asian Pear Sparkler

You can substitute the Asian pear with normal pear.

Preparation time: 10 minutes

Cooking time: 15 minutes

Servings: 6

Ingredients:

1 cup of Asian pear juice, freshly pressed

¼ cup of sugar

¾ cup of honey

1 teaspoon of lemon juice

Soda water

1 piece of fresh ginger, peeled and cut into coins

1 sprig of fresh rosemary

Little grating of fresh nutmeg

Ice

Directions:

1. In a saucepan, mix all the ingredients except the soda and ice. Bring to boil over medium heat. Reduce the heat and simmer on low for 5 minutes while stirring continuously so that the sugar can dissolve. Remove from heat and leave to sit for 30 minutes

2. Through a fine-mesh strainer, strain the mixture and dispose of the solids. Allow to completely cool.

3. Fill an 8-ounce glass with ice cubes halfway, add 3 tablespoons of the cooled syrup, fill with the soda water and stir.

Cucumber Mojito

The teetotalers version of the famous mojito.

Preparation time: 10 minutes

Cooking time: 0 minute

Servings: 1

Ingredients:

4 ounces of club soda

1 tablespoon of white sugar

3-4 sprigs of fresh mint leaves

Juice of ½ a lime

½ lime, cut into wedges

Ice

½ cucumber, peeled and pureed

Directions:

1. In a food processor, puree the cucumber with lime juice and pour into an ice-filled glass.

2. Muddle the mint, lime wedges and sugar and add it to the glass along with the club soda.

Rosemary Cranberry Refresher

Sweet and savory.

Preparation time: 5 minutes

Cooking time: 5 minutes

Servings 4

Ingredients:

1 pound of fresh cranberries, juiced

3 fresh sprigs of rosemary plus extra to garnish

2 cups of water

4 apples, juiced

Ice

Directions:

1. Boil water in a small pot or covered saucepan. Add the rosemary sprigs, turn down heat and leave to simmer for 5 minutes. Remove pot from heat and leave to steep for an hour while covered. Keep chilled in refrigerator until it is time to serve.

2. Mix the cranberry and apple juice with the rosemary water.

3. Garnish with the rosemary sprigs and serve over ice.

Sangria

Makes for a nice party punch.

Preparation time: 12 minutes

Cooking time: 0 minute

Servings: 8

Ingredients:

3 cups of pomegranate juice

3 cups of carbonated water

2 cups of boiling water

1 cup of orange juice, freshly squeezed

½ cup of sugar

1 medium-sized lemon, sliced into thin rounds

1 medium-sized orange, sliced into thin rounds

1 medium-sized apple, cored and cut into chunks of ½-inches

1 medium-sized lime, sliced into thin rounds

2 cinnamon sticks

2 black tea bags

Directions:

1. Add the boiling water to the tea bags and cinnamon sticks. Leave to steep for 5 minutes. Remove the tea bags, add the sugar and stir until it dissolves.

2. Mix the rest of the ingredients except the carbonated water, in a large pitcher or jar. Keep in the refrigerator for an hour or overnight, preferably.

3. Stir in the carbonated water just before serving and pour into glasses containing ice.

Roy Rodgers

Terribly cool to drink.

Preparation time: 5 minutes

Cooking time: 0 minute

Servings: 2

Ingredients:

1 tablespoon grenadine

1 bottle or can Coca Cola

Maraschino cherry, optional

Directions:

1. Add coke to an ice-filled glass.

2. Add grenadine and stir.

3. Garnish with cherry.

Non-alcoholic Margaritas

Frozen margaritas without alcohol.

Preparation time: 10 minutes

Cooking time: 0 minute

Servings: 8

Ingredients:

4 cups of ice cubes

¾ cup of orange juice

2/3 cup of unsweetened grapefruit juice

1 (6-oz) can of frozen limeade concentrate

Lime wedge

Coarse sugar

Directions:

1. Use the lime wedge to rub the edge of margarita glasses. Dip the rims of the glasses in coarse sugar.

2. Blend the remaining ingredients until they are slushy. Pour in the margarita glasses and serve.

Moscow Mule Mocktail

Still packs a lot of punch.

Preparation time: 5 minutes

Cooking time: 0 minute

Servings: 1

Ingredients:

2 ounces of club soda, or sparkling water or tonic

1 ounce of lime juice

½ cup of ginger beer

1 tablespoon of simple syrup

Ice cubes

Directions:

1. Pour all the ingredients in a glass. Stir thoroughly.

2. Garnish with a lime slice or ginger slice.

The Palauxma

Perfect for hot summer nights.

Preparation time: 7 minutes

Cooking time: 0 minute

Servings: 2

Ingredients:

½ cup of grapefruit juice, freshly squeezed

¼ `cup of lime juice, freshly squeezed

¾ cup of club soda

2 small glasses of ice

4 drops liquid stevia

For , garnish, grapefruit or lime wedges

Directions:

1. In a large glass or shaker, combine the juices with the stevia.

2. Share the club soda among 2 glasses containing ice.

3. Divide the juice mixture among each glasses.

4. Garnish with the grapefruit or lime wedges.

BAR SNACKS

Roasted Chickpeas

This snack will have you crunching all day at the beach.

Preparation time: 15 minutes

Cooking time: 45 minutes

Servings: 3

Ingredients:

1 can 15-ounce of chickpeas, drained

¼ teaspoon of ground coriander

¼ teaspoon of chili pepper powder

¼ teaspoon of garlic powder

¼ teaspoon of ground cumin

¼ teaspoon of curry powder

¼ teaspoon of paprika

1/8 teaspoon of kosher salt

Olive oil spray

Directions:

1. Preheat oven to 375°F.

2. In a colander, drain the chickpeas and allow to completely dry.

3. Arrange the dried chickpeas on a baking sheet in a single layer. Put in the oven and roast for about 35-45 minutes until they are crunchy on the inside and golden brown on the outside.

4. Combine all the spices in a medium bowl. Remove the roasted chickpeas from oven, spray with olive oil and toss `with the spices while they are hot.

Date Almond Balls

Super easy to prepare.

Preparation time: 20 minutes

Cooking time: 0 minute

Servings: 24

Ingredients:

1¼ cup of dates, chopped and pitted

1¼ cup of gluten-free rolled oats

½ cup of unsalted unsweetened almond butter

1 teaspoon of pure almond extract

¼ teaspoon of ground nutmeg

¼ teaspoon of ground ginger

Directions:

1. In a food processor, process all the ingredients together until they are sticky and smooth. Add 2-3 tablespoons of hot water to enable the mixture form a ball.

2. Scoop a heaping spoonful of the mixture with a teaspoon and roll into a ball. Press firmly while rolling so that it sticks together. Chill before serving.

Baked Sweet Potato Chips

Enjoy a day in the sands with this delicious snack.

Preparation time: 10 minutes

Cooking time: 20 minutes

Servings: 8-10

Ingredients:

1½ pounds of sweet potatoes

1/3 cup of olive oil

Kosher Salt

Directions:

1. Preheat oven to 400°F.

2. Use parchment paper to line several baking sheets and keep aside.

3. Cut the potatoes into paper-tin rounds with a mandolin slicer.

4. Put the cut potatoes in a bowl and drizzle oil over the top. Toss gently to coat every of the potato with oil. Set the potatoes in a single layer on the prepared baking sheets.

5. Sprinkle salt on chips lightly. Put in oven and bake for 20-25 minutes until it is golden around the edges and crispy.

Almond Vanilla Snack Bars

A healthy snack devoid of extra calories.

Preparation time: 10 minutes (plus cooling time)

Cooking time: 20 minutes

Servings: 12

Ingredients:

1 1/3 cups of whole almonds, roughly chopped

¼ cup of almond meal

1/3 cup of brown rice syrup or honey

¾ cup of salted sunflower seeds

1 tablespoon of almond butter

5 Medjool dates, roughly chopped

1 teaspoon of vanilla extract

1/8 teaspoon of salt

Directions:

1. Preheat oven to 300°F.

2. Use a parchment paper to line a baking sheet. Keep aside.

3. Combine the vanilla, salt, almond meal, honey and almond butter thoroughly. Then fold in the chopped almonds, sunflower seeds and dates.

4. Put this mixture in the baking sheet and press into an even layer very firmly. Put in oven and bake for 20 minutes.

5. Remove from oven, allow to completely cool on the wire rack for an hour before chilling in the refrigerator for an extra hour.

6. Remove and cut into bars.

Nutella Brownies

An easy option for a day at the beach.

Preparation time: 5 minutes

Cooking time: 15 minutes

Servings: 5

Ingredients:

1¼ cups of nutella

½ cup of all-purpose flour

2 large eggs

Directions:

1. Preheat oven to 350°F and grease a baking pan.

2. Mix all the ingredients in a large bowl until it forms a smooth batter. Pour the batter into the baking sheet and smooth the top with a spatula.

3. Bake for about 15 minutes or until a toothpick inserted in it comes out clean.

Pineapple Ice

Cool down on a hot day with this yummy snack.

Preparation time: 3 minutes

Cooking time: 0 minute

Servings: 3

Ingredients:

1 can 20-ounce of pineapple chunks in juice, chilled and undrained

2 tablespoons of fresh mint, coarsely chopped

Fresh mint sprigs, optional

Directions:

1. Keep aside 3 pineapple chunks to use as garnish.

2. In a pan, pour the remaining pineapple and its juice. Cover and keep in freezer for 1½ -2 hours or until it is almost frozen.

3. Add the frozen pineapple to a food processor and process with the mint until it is smooth but not melting. Serve garnished with sprigs of mint and reserved pineapple.

Frozen Yogurt Blueberries

Extremely yummy and delicious.

Preparation time: 10 minutes

Cooking time: 0 minute

Servings: 2

Ingredients:

1 6-ounce container of fresh blueberries

1 6-ounce container of nonfat blueberry Greek yogurt

Directions:

1. Line a baking pan with wax or parchment paper. Wash the blueberries.

2. Dip each blueberry into the yogurt with a toothpick and swirl to coat. Set in baking pan. Repeat process for the other blueberries.

3. Freeze baking pan for an hour at least.

Peanut Butter Banana Ice Cream
No day at the beach is complete without ice cream.

Preparation time: 10 minutes

Cooking time: 0 minute

Servings: 4

Ingredients:

4 ripe and large bananas, peeled and sliced into ½-in discs

2 tablespoons of peanut butter

Directions

1. Arrange the sliced banana on a baking pan or large plate in a single layer. Keep in freezer for 1-2 hours.

2. Process the frozen banana in a blender or food processor until it is smooth and creamy. Add in the peanut butter and continue processing to mix.

3. Keep in freezer for a few hours before serving.

Spicy Popcorn

Keep the party popping with this super spicy snack.

Preparation time: 5 minutes

Cooking time: 20 minutes

Servings: 4-6

Ingredients:

½ cup of popcorn kernels

3 tablespoons of canola oil

2-3 tablespoons of butter

1-2 teaspoons of kosher salt

1-2 teaspoons of sriracha

Directions:

1. Use the oil to grease the bottom of a large pot. Add the popcorn kernels, cover and set over medium-high heat.

2. Shake the pot when the kernels begin to pop. Do this until all the kernels pops.

3. Remove from heat when there are no more popping sounds and transfer to a big bowl.

4. Meanwhile, melt the butter; mix with the sriracha and stir.

5. Drizzle this butter mixture over the popcorn, toss and season with salt.

The End

Made in the USA
Middletown, DE
25 September 2018